FESTIVE Cakes of CHRISTMAS

Norma Jost Voth

Illustrated by Ellen Jane Price

HERALD PRESS
Scottdale, Pennsylvania
Waterloo, Ontario

Library of Congress Cataloging in Publication Data

Voth, Norma Jost.
    Festive cakes of Christmas.

    1. Cake. 2. Christmas cookery. I. Title.
TX771.V67   641.8'653   81-2140
ISBN 0-8361-1956-8 (pbk.)   AACR2

FESTIVE CAKES OF CHRISTMAS
Copyright © 1981 by Herald Press, Scottdale, Pa. 15683
    Published simultaneously in Canada by Herald Press,
    Waterloo, Ont. N2L 6H7. All rights reserved.
Library of Congress Catalog Card Number: 81-2140
International Standard Book Number: 0-8361-1956-8
Printed in the United States of America

96 95 94 93 92 91   10 9 8 7 6 5

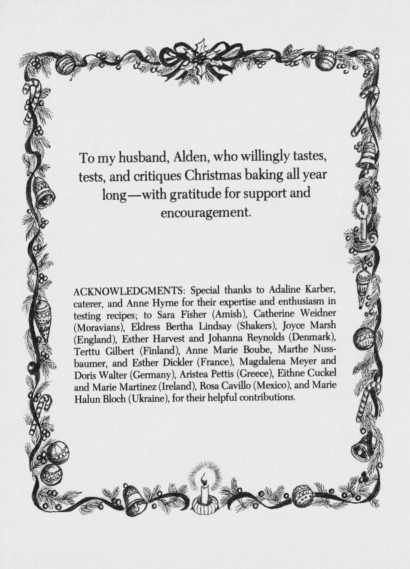

To my husband, Alden, who willingly tastes, tests, and critiques Christmas baking all year long—with gratitude for support and encouragement.

ACKNOWLEDGMENTS: Special thanks to Adaline Karber, caterer, and Anne Hyrne for their expertise and enthusiasm in testing recipes; to Sara Fisher (Amish), Catherine Weidner (Moravians), Eldress Bertha Lindsay (Shakers), Joyce Marsh (England), Esther Harvest and Johanna Reynolds (Denmark), Terttu Gilbert (Finland), Anne Marie Boube, Marthe Nussbaumer, and Esther Dickler (France), Magdalena Meyer and Doris Walter (Germany), Aristea Pettis (Greece), Eithne Cuckel and Marie Martinez (Ireland), Rosa Cavillo (Mexico), and Marie Halun Bloch (Ukraine), for their helpful contributions.

In earlier times the season of Christmas was long, stretching from St. Thomas' Day—when cooks begin in earnest to prepare their plum puddings—to the blessing of the candles on Candlemas. In Scandinavia, the Danes still celebrate "the month of Christmas."

Indeed, it is more than a hurried day or two. Christmas is a season, a holy festival to be celebrated and savored, to be held long enough to feel the deep, moving significance of this holy time.

And who can keep such a time of festivity without good food? The feeling that good food is necessary to make a good festival has long been with us. Carols sing of it, ballads list delicacies to be eaten for the celebration. Probably more tasty foods and lovely pastries are prepared for the feast of Christmas than any other.

In these pages is a collection of hallowed traditions, anecdotes, and fanciful cakes and tarts typical of the season, gathered from many countries. May they add richness to your own family's cherished traditions.

The Christmas Season

From Advent to Candlemas

Advent

Advent begins with the fourth Sunday before Christmas. These four weeks are a time of spiritual preparation, heralding the coming of Christ into the world.

"Prepare the way of the Lord" (Matthew 3:3).

European children eagerly count the long days before Christmas by opening tiny numbered doors on Advent calendars. Inside are secret pictures, little messages, or even small presents.

Advent wreaths, fashioned of evergreens and decorated with four candles, hang in living rooms and adorn dining tables throughout Northern Europe. Each Advent Sunday a candle is lighted—until all are burning—making it a lovely time for family and friends to gather around the wreath to sing the old Advent songs and sample the first Christmas cookies.

For European homemakers, Advent is a busy season of cleaning, baking, and preparing for the holiday. German women, especially, take great pains with their *Weihnachts Gebäck* (Christmas baking).

Everywhere these four weeks before Christmas are looked upon as a preparation for the greatest festival of the Christian year.

8

St. Nicholas' Day

December 6, St. Nicholas' Day for European children is the time for presents. In Holland, Sint Nikolaas, as he is called there, arrives in harbor cities by boat and is greeted by the mayor and cheered by thousands of children and adults. He rides into the city on horseback, dressed in a white robe and bishop's golden mitre. With him are *swarte pieten* (servants) wearing puffed breeches and plumed hats. One carries a bag of presents, peppernuts, cookies, and a birch rod. In Amsterdam they lead a parade to the royal palace.

On St. Nikolaas Eve Dutch children put out hay and carrots for the good saint's horse and neatly set their shoes before the fireplace, hoping for gifts. But, if Katy has been lazy or young Diedrich impolite, St. Nikolaas knows all—and *Swarte Piet* (Black Peter) leaves a birch switch instead of sweets.

Fact and legend mix, but there actually was a generous Bishop Nikolaos, born in Patara, Turkey, more than 1,700 years ago. He left a wealthy home to serve the church and was known as a loving, compassionate man who helped the poor. It is said he remembered needy children with gifts on their door-steps at night, without them knowing where the presents came from.

Europe celebrates his day and remembers his kind deeds by giving gifts.

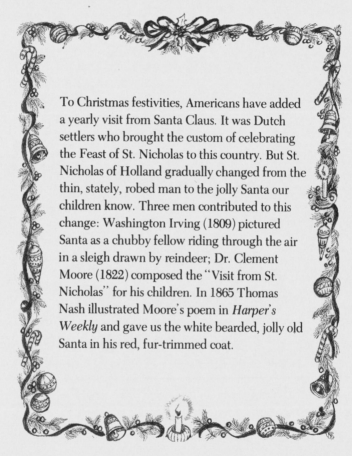

To Christmas festivities, Americans have added a yearly visit from Santa Claus. It was Dutch settlers who brought the custom of celebrating the Feast of St. Nicholas to this country. But St. Nicholas of Holland gradually changed from the thin, stately, robed man to the jolly Santa our children know. Three men contributed to this change: Washington Irving (1809) pictured Santa as a chubby fellow riding through the air in a sleigh drawn by reindeer; Dr. Clement Moore (1822) composed the "Visit from St. Nicholas" for his children. In 1865 Thomas Nash illustrated Moore's poem in *Harper's Weekly* and gave us the white bearded, jolly old Santa in his red, fur-trimmed coat.

St. Lucia's Day

December 13, St. Lucia's Day, is celebrated in Scandinavia, and especially Sweden, as "The Feast of Light." Every Swedish home has a lovely early morning Lucia ceremony.

Up before dawn, the eldest daughter of the family is Lucia for the day. She dons a flowing white gown and wears a crown of lingenberry leaves with white candles on her head. Carrying a tray of steaming coffee and fragrant golden saffron buns and *pepparkakor*, Lucia goes from room to room singing Lucia songs and wakening the family with breakfast in bed.

Every school, village, and city has its Lucia Queen who presides over parades or day-long festivities.

Lucia's legend came to Sweden from Italy and honors a fourth-century girl who died a Christian martyr after distributing her dowry to the poor on the eve of her wedding. In Italy, Lucia is remembered with bonfires and torchlight parades.

Christmas Eve

December 24 is Christmas Eve or Holy Evening. In many countries shops and stores close by midafternoon. Streets are deserted and silent while families gather at home to celebrate the humble birth of Christ in a stable in Bethlehem.

Every country has its Christmas Eve rituals, but none more than Poland. At dusk, children watch anxiously for the first star to appear. Only then may the Christmas Eve supper with its twelve symbolic dishes begin. Before eating, Polish fathers share *oplateks*, rice wafers blessed by the priest. Each family member, from oldest to youngest, is greeted with a special Christmas wish.

In Ireland, tall candles glow from every window on Christmas Eve, lighting the traveler to Bethlehem.

Townspeople and choirs in the tiny Alpine village of Oberndorf, Austria, celebrate the anniversary of "Silent Night" outside the chapel where Franz Gruber played the organ (1818).

All over the world, worshipers gather at midnight church services to hear again the familiar Christmas story and sing carols of Jesus' birth.

December 24–25 was declared officially to be the birth of Christ by proclamation of Pope Julius I, in the year 350. It coincided with the time of the winter solstice, the season of the Roman Saturnalia.

Christmas Day, December 25

And Joseph . . . went up from Galilee, from the city of Nazareth, to Judea, to the city of David, which is called Bethlehem . . . to be enrolled with Mary, his betrothed, who was with child. And while they were there, the time came for her to be delivered. And she gave birth to her first-born son and wrapped him in swaddling cloths, and laid him in a manger, because there was no place for them in the inn. Luke 2:4-7.

Boxing Day

December 26, Boxing Day in England, comes from the old custom of putting money in small boxes for servants, the postman, milkman, and the like.

A century ago, when English village streets were very narrow, it was customary for tradespeople to walk though the streets with their boxes attached to long poles, making it convenient for people to drop gifts of money.

Traditionally, these gift boxes were made of metal, cardboard, or papier-mâché in shapes of squares or hexagons, and were distinguished by a generous, inviting slit. Antique boxes may still be found in British museums.

Today businesses close on Boxing Day, providing a time for the British to watch rugby, to see a pantomime (usually a children's fairy tale) in a London theater, to visit relatives, entertain, or go fox hunting in the country.

St. Stephen's Day

December 26, St. Stephen's Day in Ireland, honors Stephen, the first Christian martyr. Earlier it was known as "Wrenning Day," a time when they stoned a wren in commemoration of this saint. In some counties, children go about in costume, asking for "help to bury the wren."

This also is a day for children's pantomimes in large downtown theaters.

In other European countries, December 26 is the Second Day of Christmas, a time to begin a round of visits to friends and relatives. Christmas trees are not brought into the home until December 24, so the rest of the week is given to parties and family gatherings. Little work is done. "Christmas seems to hold on a little longer there," says Marie Martinez, of her childhood in Ireland.

New Year's Eve and Day

December 31 & January 1. On New Year's Eve and Day churches may hold "watch night services," with hymns, prayers, and communion.

For most people, this is a time of new resolutions, with lists of ways to make the coming year better. At midnight bells toll, fireworks may light the sky, and people go about wishing each other a happy new year.

In Holland, Dutch women stir up batches of Olliebollen—fat golden raisin fritters—to serve with pots of hot coffee on New Year's Day.

THE FEAST OF ST. BASIL is celebrated in Greek Orthodox churches on New Year's Day. Presents are given on this day, rather than on Christmas. Basil, one of the great fathers of the Catholic and Orthodox churches, is remembered for founding orphanages, hospitals, and schools. A handsome cake, *Vasilopita* (St. Basil's cake, p.76), is brought to the church and blessed in a vesper ceremony. At the stroke of midnight (New Year's Eve) the *Vasilopita*, baked with a hidden fortune coin inside, is served according to old ritual.

The Feast of Epiphany

January 6, The Feast of Epiphany or *Little Christmas*, is a holy festival honoring the wise men coming to the infant Jesus.

> And lo, the star, which they saw in the east, went
> before them, till it came and stood over where
> the young child was. When they saw the star,
> they rejoiced with exceeding great joy.
> *Matt. 2:9b–11.*

This day is also known as *Three Kings' Day, Feast of the Magi,* and *Twelfth Night,* the traditional English Name—the twelfth night after Christmas.

For many Eastern rite churches, this day commemorates the baptism of Jesus in a special service. If there is a nearby body of water, the priest may lead a procession to a lake or river for the "Blessing of the Water." Some Eastern churches still celebrate Epiphany according to the old Julian calendar, which falls on our January 18.

Polish people write the letters KMB above their doorways to remind all who enter of the coming of the wise men.

In Italy, Epipany is called *Old Christmas* and gifts are exchanged. Children hang their stockings and wait for the good witch, *Le Befana,* to bring their toys.

Epiphany usually marks the close of the twelve days of Christmas.

St. Knut's Day

January 13, St. Knut's Day in Scandinavia, ends the Yule season and a month of Christmas. In Sweden the tree is dismantled and children may choose a prize of cookies or candy from the decorations. Carols are sung and there is a last dance around the tree. With singing and much laughter, the tree is taken out the door with the wish:

> May God bless your Christmas.
> May it last till Easter.

Candlemas Day

February 2, Candlemas Day. Many years ago the Feast of Purification of the Virgin (a ritual required by Jewish law 40 days after the birth of a child) was chosen by the Pope as a day for the blessing of candles people carried in processions before mass. The day is observed in Greek, Roman Catholic, and Protestant Episcopal churches.

In Mexico, the person who finds a large bean or china doll in his slice of Three Kings' Cake (January 6) must host a party on Candlemas.

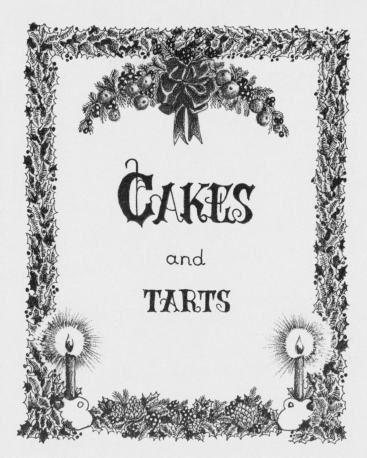

CAKES

and

TARTS

A special kind of excitement filled Mother's kitchen in late November—there was a new feeling of warmth, a kind of spicy expectancy of good things to come.

Evenings when a cold, blustery wind howled outside were perfect for sorting through the recipe box and thumbing through the old, hand-written cookbook with its pages of fruit cake and honey cookies recipes.

There were cozy times of sitting at the oak table helping chop fruit and raisins, cracking and shelling nuts, and crushing fresh spices in the grinder. Some evenings there were bowls brimming with fruit to be mixed with a fragrant batter, crocks to be packed with dough to age and mellow before baking.

Best of all were the times when the first baking came from the oven and we welcomed cookies slightly burned or shaved off tiny slivers of fruit cake. Later there would be evenings with chairs pulled up to the kitchen table to celebrate the Christmas baking with a fresh table cloth, a lighted candle, and a steaming pot of coffee.

Indeed, Christmas baking was special, for those were delicacies to be baked and eaten only once a year.

Yule Cake

Lavishly studded with colorful fruits and whole nuts, this recipe, from a former neighbor, Thelma Luckenbill, Upland, California, is a family favorite.

1½ cups Brazil nuts, whole
1½ cups walnut halves
1 cup pitted dates
1 cup candied orange peel, chopped
½ cup candied red cherries
½ cup candied green cherries
½ cup seedless raisins
¾ cup flour
¾ cup sugar
½ tsp. baking powder
½ tsp. salt
3 eggs
1 tsp. vanilla

Grease 9×5×3-inch loaf pan; line bottom with parchment. Place fruit and nuts in large bowl. Sift dry ingredients over fruit and mix well. Beat eggs until light; add vanilla. Blend into fruit mixture. Spoon into loaf pan; spread evenly. Bake at 300° for 2 hours or until firm. Brush with Karo syrup to glaze. Cool 10 minutes in pan. Remove and cool on rack. Store in foil to age.

Lil's Light Fruit Cake

Lillian Proceviat has a wide repertoire of Ukrainian/American Christmas baking specialties, but this is her family's favorite cake. "My children don't care for citron, so I make this cake for them."

1 cup sweet butter	2½ cups flour
1 cup sugar	½ cup red maraschino
5 eggs	cherries, diced
¼ tsp. mace	½ cup green maraschino
1 tsp. vanilla or ½	cherries, diced
tsp. almond extract	½ cup pecans, coarsely
	chopped

Bring butter and eggs to room temperature. Sift flour and measure. Drain, chop, and dry cherries on paper towels. In one cup of the flour, dredge cherries and pecans; shake off excess flour and retain for cake. Cream butter and sugar until light and fluffy. Add eggs, one at a time, beating hard after each addition. Add spice and flavoring. (Mrs. Proceviat also suggests ¼ cup rum or brandy as an alternate.) Mix well.

Add flour, a small amount at a time, using flour from fruit and nuts. Beat hard until batter is smooth. Gently fold in fruit and nuts, spreading colors of cherries evenly. Spoon batter into greased and floured loaf pan. Bake at 275° for 1½ hours or until done. Cool on rack. Brush with glaze. Decorate with candied cherries and whole pecans. Store in foil.

—*Mrs. Proceviat is the owner of The Kiev Kitchen, Mountain View, California.*

New England Cranberry Tarts

3 cups cranberries	1 tbsp. orange rind, grated
½ cup raisins	1 cup water
1½ cups sugar	Topping
2 tbsp. cornstarch	Pastry 2 crust, 9-inch pie

Prepare pie crust pastry and chill. Cut 10–12 circles with 4½ inch cutter. Press circles into tart or 2½-inch muffin pans. In saucepan combine cranberries, raisins, orange rind and water. Simmer 3 minutes. Mix together sugar and cornstarch; stir into cranberries. Cook and stir until thick and bubbly. Spoon into tart shells. Combine ¾ cup flour, ⅓ cup sugar; cut in 6 tbsp. butter until crumbly. Sprinkle over tarts. Bake at 400° for about 15–20 minutes or until golden brown.

Hal Bohannon's Chocolate Spice Cake

A luscious chocolate chiffon cake, topped with whipped cream, makes an elegant addition to a New Year's buffet. The recipe comes from the menu of the old Bohannon Restaurant, well know in San Jose, California. After retiring, Mr. Bohannon taught cooking classes in this area, sharing his secrets, recipes, and skills from a lifetime of good cooking.

½ cup sweet chocolate, ground
¾ cup boiling water
1½ cups flour
1¾ cups sugar
4 tsp. baking powder
¾ tsp. salt
2 tsp. allspice
1 tsp. cinnamon
7 eggs, separated
½ cup salad oil
2 tsp. orange peel, grated
½ tsp. cream of tartar
1 cup walnuts, finely chopped
Whipping cream

Stir chocolate and boiling water until dissolved and smooth. Cool. Sift together flour, 1½ cups sugar, baking powder, salt, allspice, and cinnamon. Make a well in the dry ingredients and add egg yolks, oil, orange peel, and chocolate mix. Stir until smooth. Beat egg whites until foamy, add cream of tartar, and gradually beat in remaining sugar. Beat to stiff peak stage and gently fold into the chocolate mixture. Sprinkle nuts on top and fold in. Bake in an ungreased 10-inch tube pan at 350° for about 1 hour. Invert pan and cool. Frost with chocolate butter-cream or whipped cream.

To decorate with whipped cream, cut a well or "trench" 1 inch wide and 1 inch deep in the top of the cake. Scoop out pieces of cake from well. Fill with whipped cream. Fill pastry bag with remaining cream and using Open Star Pastry Tube #1 make swirls over the filled well and around the base of the cake with whipped cream. Top the swirls with 8-10 drained long-stemmed red maraschino cherries.

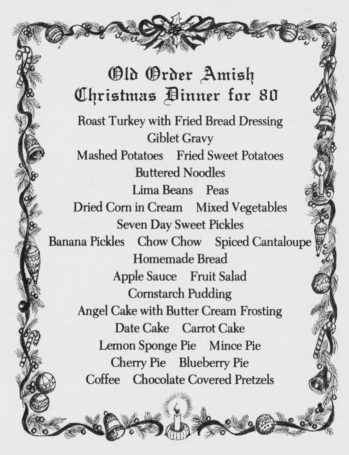

Old Order Amish Christmas Dinner for 80

Roast Turkey with Fried Bread Dressing
Giblet Gravy
Mashed Potatoes   Fried Sweet Potatoes
Buttered Noodles
Lima Beans   Peas
Dried Corn in Cream   Mixed Vegetables
Seven Day Sweet Pickles
Banana Pickles   Chow Chow   Spiced Cantaloupe
Homemade Bread
Apple Sauce   Fruit Salad
Cornstarch Pudding
Angel Cake with Butter Cream Frosting
Date Cake   Carrot Cake
Lemon Sponge Pie   Mince Pie
Cherry Pie   Blueberry Pie
Coffee   Chocolate Covered Pretzels

"In our family it is common to have 80 guests or more for Christmas dinner," says Sara Fisher, who grew up in an Old Order Amish home. "Married family, children, aunts, uncles, grandparents, all are invited. But then, our homes are built to accommodate 200 people for church services, so we are set up for big groups.

"Long before Christmas the ladies get together to plan the menu and what to bring. Guests always 'sit up to tables' and dinner is served in sittings—the older men first, then younger men and boys. Little boys under six sit with their fathers. Young mothers and girls serve, and the table is set and respread in a short time.

"When the dishes are done, we gather in the living room to sing the old German Christmas hymns until it is time to go home. Before leaving, there is a snack of cookies and coffee."

Amish women are known for their good Pennsylvania-Dutch style cooking; the men are industrious, thrifty farmers. The Amish teach separation from the world, personal simplicity. Some groups farm with horses and live without electricity, telephones, and autos.

—Sara Fisher is a teacher in an Old Order Amish school near Soudersburg, Pennsylvania

27

Amish Date-Nut Cake

Popular among Amish families in the Lancaster area of Pennsylvania, this cake, served with whipped cream, makes a nice substitute for traditional fruit cake.

1 pound walnut meats, coarsely chopped	2 tsp. baking powder
1 pound dates, chopped	1 cup sugar
1 cup flour	4 eggs, separated
½ tsp. salt	1 tsp. vanilla
	Glaze

Place dates and nuts in large bowl; sift dry ingredients over fruit and nuts. Blend well. Stir in well-beaten egg yolks and vanilla. Beat egg whites until stiff peaks form. Fold into batter. Pour into greased 9×5×3-inch loaf pan. Bake at 350° for about 1½ hours or until done. Brush with Karo syrup while hot. Decorate with candied cherries and blanched almonds. Cool in pan 10 minutes. Serve with whipped cream.

Moravian Christmas

In Moravian Communities it is the tradition to go *putzing* during the Christmas season. Homes are open to visitors, so families drop in on their friends to admire each other's Christmas *putz* (crèche).

For many years the Moravians have used these manger scenes as a beautiful way of telling the Christmas story to children, their neighbors, and friends. Sometimes a whole room is given over to the *putz*, which is often built on a raised platform. Moss, rocks, old tree stumps, and evergreens form a background for beautiful hand-carved wooden figures from Germany. Whenever visitors come in, a member of the family reads the Christmas story.

The word *putz*, which means "to decorate," comes from a German dialect.

Moravians in the Christmas city of Bethlehem, Pennsylvania, also decorate a large community *putz* at the Central Moravian Church, attracting thousands of visitors each December. Neighborhoods all over that city glow with single lighted candles in windows of Moravian (and other) homes from the first Sunday of Advent throughout the Christmas season.

Moravian Sugar Cake (p. 30) is served at home and at church meetings during the holidays and all through the year.

29

Catherine Weidner's Moravian Sugar Cake

Originally made by the early settlers, Moravian Sugar Cake is served at weddings, social affairs, and holidays in the Bethlehem, Pennsylvania, area. Catherine Weidner, who is married to Pastor Mervin Weidner of Central Moravian Church in Bethlehem, shares her family recipe.

1 pkg. active dry yeast	½ tsp. salt
1 cup warm potato water	6-7 cups flour
1 cup sugar	1 lb. light brown
½ cup shortening	sugar
½ cup butter or margarine	½ cup butter
3 eggs, beaten	Cinnamon, nutmeg
1 cup warm mashed	Evaporated milk
potatoes	

Pare, slice, and boil 2 or 3 potatoes. Drain (saving water) and mash. Cool to lukewarm. Sprinkle yeast in 1 cup potato water; dissolve. Cream shortening, butter, and sugar until fluffy. Add eggs and mix well. Add potatoes, salt, yeast and warm potato water and mix. Gradually add about 3-3½ cups flour and beat 5 minutes with electric mixer. Gradually add 3 more cups flour. Turn out on floured board and knead until smooth and elastic, about 8-10 minutes. Place dough in greased bowl, turning to grease top. Cover with kitchen towel and set in warm place until double in bulk (about 1½-2 hours). Punch down and knead lightly.

Divide dough into 4 pieces and pat into 4 greased 9×9-inch pans (or 2 large rectangular pans). Cover and let rise in warm place until light and puffy, but not quite double. With thumb, make indentations in cakes and push small pieces of butter into holes. Cover entire top with light brown sugar; then sprinkle with cinnamon and a bit of nutmeg. Repeat on each cake. Dot with more butter. Drizzle lightly with evaporated milk or cream. Bake at 350° for about 20 minutes or until golden brown. Cool. Serve warm.

The Moravian Christmas Putz

Shaker Christmas

Early Shakers celebrated Christmas as a time of giving and forgiving. Not only was their communal dwelling to be polished and scrubbed for this holy day, but the sisters and brothers were to "sweep the house of the spirit," and "wash from the floor the stains of sin," sometimes using imaginary mops and brooms. All members were to make reconciliation, leave grudges behind, remember the poor, and keep the day sacred. For the children, there were imaginary gifts often accompanied by pantomime— "cakes of love," "gold of golden plums," and "clusters of grapes filled with the love of God."

—From the Shaker Order of Christmas.

Sister Lucy Ann's Christmas Cake

Sister Lucy Ann Shepard's spice cake is included in a little book of *Shaker Tested Recipes* from the Canterbury Village in New Hampshire. Eldress Bertha Lindsay fondly remembers Lucy Ann "as a beautiful sister, involved in the ministry, and a trustee of our group." She must have enjoyed a turn in the kitchen as well, making Christmas cake.

1 cup butter	1 tsp. cinnamon
1 cup sugar	1 cup candied fruits or
6 eggs	citron, chopped
1¾ cups flour	1 cup currants
1½ tsp. baking powder	½ cup orange juice or
1 tsp. allspice	apple juice

Cream butter and sugar until light and fluffy. Add eggs, one at a time, beating well. Sift dry ingredients together and add to batter. Drain fruits and dredge in flour; shake off excess. Add fruits and orange juice to batter; mix thoroughly. Pour into well-greased and floured tube pan. Bake at 350° for 1 hour or until done.

Cool. Store in foil. Before serving, glaze with powdered sugar and lemon juice. Decorate with candied cherries. (Sister Lucy Ann used brandy in place of orange juice in her cake.)

33

Christmas at Canterbury Village

Shaker Eldress, Bertha Lindsay, remembers Christmases at the Canterbury Village (New Hampshire) when the choir came into the dining room singing carols Christmas morning. "We started in the attic, and made our way down to the dining room in two groups, singing all the way, meeting at our tables.

"The sisters used to have their little rooms festooned with red and green and white, and the children's workshop was always festive with greenery and presents. One year we had a peach tree with stuffed birds. We made simple gifts for our teachers and sisters.

"Each year I wrote a letter to the sister who took care of me. Bible stories were dramatized in the chapel on Christmas Eve, and Christmas Day, after a lovely dinner of turkey and 'all the fixings,' we just enjoyed our presents."

Dedicated to hard work, thrift, and celibacy, Shakers wore plain clothes and led quiet lives in communal villages. They made outstanding contributions to simple furniture design and agricultural advancement. "Give your hands to work and your hearts to God" was a creed they lived.

Eldress Lindsay came to the Shaker village at the age of eight, when her mother died. Now 83, she is one of the nine elderly sisters who remain from this once thriving group.

In our little country school in Kansas we always had a Christmas program, Helen Epp of Newton, Kansas, reminisces. It was thrilling to have a tree with real candles and watch the older men guard it with wet cotton on long sticks. We gladly took the job of stringing popcorn and cranberries for the tree— an excuse not to do our schoolwork.

Everyone had dialogues and poems (called a *Wünsch*), to recite—sometimes more than one. The longer, the better. The more you could say, the smarter you were!

After the program there were sacks with treats. "An orange was really something precious. I always kept mine until it was about dried out—until my brother George would get so hungry for it he couldn't stand it anymore. Then I sold it to him and he gave me money for it!"

35

Silent night, Holy night

Austria's Gift to the World

A broken church organ prompted the composing of the world's most popular Christmas carol, "Silent Night." It was December 23, 1818, when Pastor Josef Mohr discovered mice had chewed holes in the bellows of the church organ. To have some music for the Christmas Eve mass, Mohr quickly wrote the words for a simple song and showed them to his good schoolmaster friend, Franz Gruber. A few hours later, Gruber had set the words to music for two voices, choir, and guitar—a "worldly" instrument never used in church before.

For the first time on December 25, the two men sang "Silent Night," accompanied only by Gruber's guitar and a small choir.

Every Christmas Eve at 5:00 p.m., the Choral Society of Oberndorf (near Salzburg in the Austrian Tyrol) sings a memorial concert around a lighted Christmas tree outside the tiny memorial chapel where this hymn was written.

Viennese Sachertorte

Served in the coffee room of the Sacher Hotel, Vienna, this simple but elegant cake was invented in 1832 by master sugar baker, Franz Sacher. A chocolate-lover's delight, *Sachertorte* (Zahk-er-tohr-teh) is a chocolate-rich sponge cake, filled or coated with apricot jam and glazed with dark, bittersweet chocolate. Viennese add a side serving of *Schlagobers*, or whipped cream.

6 oz. semi-sweet chocolate	8 egg yolks
1 cup sweet butter	1 cup flour
1 cup confectioners' sugar	10 egg whites
½ tsp. vanilla	1 cup apricot jam
	Chocolate glaze
	Whipping cream

Preheat oven to 325°. Butter two 9-inch round cake pans and line with circles of wax paper; butter and sprinkle paper with flour. Shake off excess flour. Chop chocolate into small pieces. Melt over double boiler. Cream butter; blend in sugar and vanilla. Blend in chocolate. Add egg yolks, 1 at a time, beating well after each addition. Gradually add sifted flour to chocolate mixture. With egg whites at room temperature, beat until stiff peaks form (not dry). Mix about ⅓ of egg whites into the chocolate mixture, then pour the chocolate over the remaining egg whites. Fold in with rubber spatula, using a cutting motion until no trace of white remains. Do not overfold. Pour batter into cake pans and bake 25-30 minutes at 325° or until cake is done. Remove from pans and cool.

Heat apricot jam to boiling. Strain through a fine strainer or place in blender. Place lower layer of cake on rack over a baking sheet. Spread with apricot jam. Place second layer on top. Spread top and sides with jam.

Glaze: 3 oz. unsweetened chocolate, 1 cup whipping cream, 1 cup sugar, 1 tsp. corn syrup, 1 egg, 1½ tsp. vanilla extract. Break chocolate into small pieces. In heavy saucepan combine broken pieces of chocolate, cream, sugar, and corn syrup. Cook over low heat, stirring constantly until sugar melts. Increase heat to medium and cook without stirring until a few drops of mixture form a soft ball in cold water. Beat egg lightly and stir in small amounts of chocolate, stirring rapidly. Return chocolate to saucepan and stir briskly. Cook over low heat until mixture coats wooden spoon. Add vanilla. Pour over cake, evenly coating sides. Refrigerate 3-4 hours. Remove 1 hour before serving. Offer with side serving of whipped cream.

Treasures from the Tyrol

In writing of family Christmases in their Alpine home in Austria, the Baroness Maria Von Trapp recalls a large crib placed in the living room during Advent. At first it would be empty, she says, but always there was a big bagful of straw beside it. Every evening, after prayers, each child took as many pieces of straw as he had done good deeds during the day and added them to the crib.

"When it was finally standing under the Christmas tree cradling the 'Baby wrapped in swaddling clothes,' the Holy Child seemed to smile at the children, grateful for the soft, warm bed prepared with so much love.... You may be very grown up, and even white-haired, but all during Advent you will feel the same urge to 'collect more straws for the crib'" (from "Christmas with the Trapp Family").

In many places in the snow-covered Tyrol, the darkness of Christmas Eve is brightened by hundreds of torches as village families make their way down the mountain to their little churches. The nighttime stillness is broken only by the crunching of boots across the snow, soft whispers, and the joyous songs of carolers, singing from church towers and the village square.

After mass, a warm fire, a festive supper, and their beloved *Weihnachtsbaum* (Christmas tree) welcome families at home.

The Month of Christmas

One of the things that stands out in my memory of childhood Christmases in Denmark is that things were done leisurely and over a long period of time. For *The Month of Christmas,* as December is still called in Denmark, my mother prepared a special "work calendar." One particular Christmasy task was allotted to each day.

Make Christmas cards
Make tree ornaments
Go on snow picnic to collect
    green branches
Wrap parcels for post

Wrap parcels for family
Bake pebernødder
Go to town to see
    Christmas lights
Make baskets for cookie
    presents for neighbors

What has lasted in my memory, and what I have tried to pass on to my own children, is this sense of joyous expectation without too much hectic rush and bustle, this sense of savoring *The Month of Christmas* leisurely so that no one is worn out when the time comes to celebrate the birth of Christ.—*Johanna Reynolds.*

Danish Almond Cake

Among the traditional Christmas desserts in Denmark is this tasty almond cake topped with chocolate glaze. Esther Harvest, Los Gatos, California, brought the recipe from her mother's home in Copenhagen.

1 cup butter or margarine	⅛ tsp. salt
	1 tsp. baking powder
1 cup sugar	3 tsp. almond extract
2 eggs	⅓ cup boiling water
1¼ cups flour	Chocolate glaze

Cream butter and sugar until fluffy. Add eggs and mix well. Gradually add flour sifted with baking powder and salt. Beat thoroughly. Add almond extract and boiling water. Mix well. Pour into greased 9- or 10-inch spring-form or tube pan. Bake at 350° for 30 minutes; reduce heat to 325° for last 30 minutes. Cool 10 minutes and remove from pan.

Glaze: ½ cup powdered sugar, 1 tbsp. cocoa, ¼ tsp. salt, 2 drops almond extract, 3 tsp. warm water. Decorate with whole blanched almonds.

Jule

All Christmas preparations had to be completed by noon on December 24, Christmas Eve. Shops closed, office workers went home, and soon church bells rang. After Mother's lunch of Christmas breads and her special liver pâté, we started to church. In our village in Jutland (Denmark) the Christmas service was early—at three o'clock. On the way we greeted each other with the happy words, "A blessed feast!" or "A blessed Christmas!"

Meanwhile at home the goose with its stuffing of prunes and apples sizzled in the oven. Red cabbage had been cooked days before (it is best that way), and tiny potatoes, saved for weeks just for this day, were cooked and ready to brown in caramel sauce. Dessert was traditional plain boiled rice pudding sprinkled with cinnamon sugar—not terribly popular the rest of the year, but on this night it all would be eaten, for in someone's portion was hidden an almond, and that *someone* received the "almond gift"—a marzipan (candy) pig.

After dishes were cleared, Father went to the living room to light the candles on the tree while the rest of us waited outside the door in the dark. What a sense of delicious excitement—muffled sounds from within and the smell of spruce twig singed by candle flame.

43

Then the door was thrown open and we all caught our breath. Each year it seemed unbelievable. We joined hands and walked in a circle around the tree, looking at the well-loved ornaments, the star which Mother had enjoyed as a small girl, the gently flickering candles, while we sang at the top of our voices the Christmas carols practiced since Advent. The custom of walking around the tree is an old pagan rite, perhaps, but the whole reason for Christmas was real enough to everyone as we sat on the floor listening to the story of Jesus' birth.

—*Johanna Reynolds, a former Friends Service worker in China, now living in Hong Kong.*

Nowhere is Christmas celebrated quite so warmly—or with so much light and good food—as in Denmark. On Christmas Eve the most lavish meal of the year is eaten. And after dessert, the plates of cookies and cakes are passed and the coffee pot refilled many times. *Julekage* (Yule-ah-kay-ah) is part of this tradition in Danish homes and in the home of Esther Harvest in Los Gatos, California.

Danish Julekage

1 cup milk	½ cup sugar
2 tbsp. active dry yeast	1 tsp. ground cardamom
4 cups flour	1½ cups raisins and
2 tsp. salt	citron, chopped
⅔ cup sweet butter	Topping
2 eggs	

Scald milk. Set aside; cool to lukewarm. Add yeast and dissolve. Sift 3 cups flour and salt into mixing bowl. With your hand or mixer, crumble butter (may be half margarine) into flour. Beat eggs and sugar with electric mixer. Add milk, yeast, and cardamom. Gradually beat in half the flour and butter mixture. Beat for 5 minutes. Gradually add remaining flour mixture and mix well. Mix in fruit lightly. Turn out onto floured board (using remaining 1 cup flour) and knead until smooth and satiny, 8–10 minutes.

Place in greased bowl, turning to grease top of dough. Cover and set in warm place and let rise until double in bulk (about 4 hours). Punch down; knead lightly. Pat dough into greased 9×13-inch pan. Spread with melted butter. Cover and let rise in warm place until almost double in bulk. Sprinkle with ¼ cup chopped blanched almonds and ¼ cup sugar. Bake at 350° for 30 minutes. Cool. Serve warm.

Come Stir the Pudding!

"Grandmother used to boil our Christmas pudding in the old brick copper (normally used for the weekly wash) in the far corner of her kitchen," remembers Joyce Marsh of Chandlers Ford, England. "Traditional Christmas pudding has to be boiled many hours, so the copper was scrubbed until it gleamed, ready for the long boiling. (This is what makes it so delicious—it's steamed, not baked.)

"There was even a ritual, a kind of folk custom to mixing the batter," says Joyce. "When all the fruits were in, Grandmother called to us, 'Come stir the pudding!' So we all took turns giving it a stir—clockwise, of course, for good luck. A genuine pudding will also have silver coins in it for good fortune. It used to be a threepenny or a Joey.

"Grandma ladled the batter into china basins (molds), tied them in linen cloths, and gently lowered them into the copper. The whole kitchen felt warm and steamy while the pudding cooked.

"The secret of a good plum pudding," Joyce adds, "is the long, slow cooking and the addition of a good spirit which gives it flavor and ensures good keeping. Puddings are sometimes made a month in advance and have been known to be kept a year."

STIR UP SUNDAY is the popular name for the Sunday before Advent. By tradition it was the last occasion on which Christmas cakes and puddings could be made if they were to be ready by December 25. It was called Stir Up Sunday after the Collect in the service for that day: "Stir up we beseech thee, O Lord, the wills of thy faithful people...."

o   o   o

Plum pudding began as "plum soup" centuries ago. Originally it was a porridge-like mixture made with mutton, steak, and fruits, including plums. In Old England, it was simply called "Christmas Pudding."

English Christmas Pudding

Plum pudding is the grand finale of every English Christmas. Its pungent fragrance was enough to melt even the heart of Scrooge.

> In half a minute Mrs. Cratchit entered, flushed, but smiling proudly: with the pudding blazing ... and bedight with Christmas holly stuck into the top. "Oh, what a wonderful pudding!" Bob Cratchit said.

1 cup sultanas
1 cup golden raisins
¾ cup currants
½ cup mixed candied fruit, chopped
½ cup slivered almonds
1 medium cooking apple, pared and grated
¼ lb. minced beef suet, chopped
1 tbsp. orange peel, grated
1 tsp. lemon peel, grated

2 cups fresh bread crumbs
1 cup flour
½ cup dark brown sugar
½ tsp. salt
½ tsp. soda
½ tsp. allspice
½ tsp. cinnamon
3 eggs
¼ cup apple cider
2 tbsp. orange juice
2 tbsp. lemon juice
Hard Sauce

Combine sultanas, raisins, currants, candied fruit, almonds, grated apple, suet, orange and lemon peel in a large bowl. Mix bread crumbs, flour, brown sugar, salt, soda, and spices. Stir into fruit mixture. Beat eggs until foamy; add apple juice (or you may use ¼ cup brandy), orange and lemon juices. Stir into fruit mixture. Spoon into a well-greased 1-quart china or glazed pottery mold. Cover top with circle of buttered grease-proof paper next to the pudding. Cover with foil and secure with string.

Place mold on rack in deep kettle; add 1 inch water. Heat water to boiling; reduce heat and cover kettle. Steam about 4-5 hours. Add boiling water to kettle when necessary. Remove mold from kettle. Remove foil; cool on wire rack. Wrap in foil and store in refrigerator at least 3 weeks.

To serve, steam mold on rack in covered kettle with 1 inch boiling water until heated, about 1-2 hours. Remove from kettle; cool slightly and unmold. Decorate and serve with whipped cream or brown sugar hard sauce.

Hard Sauce: Cream 6 tbsp. butter, 6 tbsp. sieved brown sugar until light and fluffy. Beat in 1 tbsp. at a time 2-3 tbsp. cream (or 2-3 tbsp. brandy) and ½ tsp. vanilla. Beat until mixture is light in color and holds shape. Spoon into serving dish. Refrigerate at least 1 hour.

Mincemeat Tartlets

Following the plum pudding at an English Christmas dinner comes a plate piled with hot little mince pies, dusted with sugar. These little tarts always have "lids."

1 cup cooking
 apples, chopped
1 cup raisins
½ cup currants
½ cup beef suet,
 chopped fine
⅓ cup mixed candied
 fruit, chopped

⅓ cup brown sugar
¼ cup almonds,
 chopped
¼ tsp. allspice
¼ tsp. cinnamon
⅛ tsp. cloves
⅓ cup apple cider
Pie crust pastry
Powdered sugar

Pare, core, and chop apples; combine with raisins, currants, suet, candied fruit, brown sugar, almonds, spices, and apple cider (⅛ cup brandy may be used in place of apple cider) in a large bowl. Cover bowl and set mincemeat in a cool place for 3-4 weeks.

Prepare pie crust pastry and chill. Roll pastry into a circle ⅛ inch thick. Cut 12 circles with 4½-inch cookie cutter. Press circles into well-greased and floured 2½-inch muffin tins, allowing ¼ inch dough above the rim.

Heat oven to 375°. Spoon 3 tbsp. mincemeat into each tart shell. Roll remaining pastry dough ⅛ inch think. Cut 12 circles with 2¾-inch cookie cutter. Place circles over filling. Seal edges and flute. Pierce tops several times with fork. Alternate topping: Cut stars with cookie cutter and fit over tops of tartlets instead of closed tops.

Bake at 375° for about 20 minutes or until crusts are golden. Cool on wire rack. Reheat before serving. Sprinkle lightly with powdered sugar before serving.

Jack Horner pie is named for the Christmas or mince pie from which the nursery rhyme character "took out a plum."

Before the Reformation the traditional shape for mince pies was oblong, representing the crib or manger. Sometimes this was covered with pastry. Puritans found this upsetting and considered it superstitious idolatry.

Dundee Cake

"Boxing day in England is the day the lord and lady of the manor used to wait on their servants and give them money in boxes for Christmas presents," says Joyce Marsh of Chandlers Ford, England. "Now we celebrate the day with a Dundee cake, which is also very traditional but not as rich as the Christmas Cake."

½ cup + 2 tbsp. butter
⅔ cup sugar
3 eggs
2 cups flour
1 tsp. baking powder
2-2½ tbsp. milk
Rind of 1 small orange, grated
Rind of 1 lemon, grated
1¼ cups sultanas or raisins
1¼ cups currants
¼ cup candied cherries, halved
¼ cup candied peel, diced
½ cup almonds, ground

Place butter and sugar in mixing bowl and cream until light and fluffy. Add eggs, 1 at a time, beating well after each addition. Gradually blend in sifted flour and baking powder. If mixture seems too dry, add milk. Carefully fold in lemon and orange peel, currants, sultanas or raisins, cherries, candied peel, ground almonds. Spoon into greased 8-inch cake pan lined with greaseproof paper. Arrange almond halves in flower patterns lightly on top of smoothed batter. Bake at 325° for about 2 hours or until the center is firm. Cool in pan. Keeps well in an airtight tin.

Before dawn on Christmas morning, the Scots were up baking cakes called sowens; *one was given to each member of the family. If it did not break, happiness would come to the owner.*

53

English Christmas Cake

Christmas cake in England is a large, round, rich, dark fruit cake served at tea time on Christmas Day. In the north of England it is covered with a layer of marzipan and perhaps a sprig of holly. In the south it becomes more elaborate with the addition of royal icing and tiny Christmas ornaments.

¾ cup each raisins, currants, and golden raisins

½ cup dried apricots, diced

1 cup fruit cake mix

¼ cup candied lemon and orange peel, diced

½ cup candied red cherries, quartered, (or candied red pineapple, chopped)

½ cup slivered almonds

½ cup butter, softened

½ cup brown sugar

3 eggs

½ cup orange juice

1 tsp. vanilla

½ tsp. each cloves, cinnamon, nutmeg

¼ tsp. soda

½ tsp. salt

1½ cups flour

Apricot jam

Marzipan

Royal icing

Soak diced apricots in warm water until soft; drain and pat dry. In a large bowl combine raisins, golden raisins, currants, fruit cake mix, peel, apricots, cherries, and nuts. Sprinkle with ¼ cup

54

of the sifted flour, tossing to coat evenly. Set aside. Cream butter and sugar until fluffy. Add eggs, one at a time, beating well. Add orange juice (traditionally, 2 tbsp. brandy are part of the liquid), vanilla (omit if using brandy), spices, and mix well. Gradually add remaining flour and soda. Stir in fruit and nuts. Spoon batter into well-greased 8-inch spring-form pan or 8×2 inch cake or pyrex pan lined with grease-proof paper.

Bake at 325° about 70–90 minutes, or until cake tester comes out clean. (To prevent over-browning or drying out, cover lightly with foil, if necessary.) Cool in pan 30 minutes. Remove to cooling rack. Wrap in plastic and foil and store in cool place at least 3 weeks. One week before Christmas brush cake with warm, sieved apricot jam and cover with marzipan. A day before Christmas, cover with royal icing (optional). Cake improves with age and may be stored several months.

Marzipan Covering: Crumble 8–10 oz. good quality almond paste and beat with electric mixer. Add ½ tsp. almond extract, 1 egg yolk, and 1–2 cups sifted powdered sugar. If necessary, knead with hands. On surface sprinkled with sifted powdered sugar, roll out half the marzipan to 8½-inch circle. Roll remaining marzipan into long strip to fit sides of cake. Brush cake with warm, sieved apricot jam. Place marzipan circle on top of cake and gently press into place. Wrap long strip around side of cake, pressing gently to secure. Trim. Wrap cake in foil and one week later frost with royal icing (optional).

Royal Icing: Combine 2 small egg whites, 2–3 tsp. glycerine (this makes icing softer), ½ tsp. lemon juice, and 1½ cups sifted powdered sugar in mixing bowl; beat hard until fluffy. Add additional 1½ cups powdered sugar; beat to stiff mixture. Spread sides and top of cake with thin layer of icing. (Cover bowl with cloth; icing dries quickly.) Remaining icing may be used to pipe decorative edging. Pipe red-tinted holiday greeting on top. Traditionally, small Christmas ornaments, such as trees, are placed on top of cake.

Good recipes are passed from friend to friend. Adaline Karber (San Jose, California) got this fruit cake recipe from her sister-in-law, Mary Martens (British Columbia), who got it from an English friend who got it from . . . !

"We always listen to the Queen's speech on Christmas day," says Joyce Marsh. "We plan our dinner before or after her message. It's tradition in most every British family to listen to her speech."

Night of the "Big Nuff"

"The afternoon of December 24, Mother always served a 'big tea'—little mince pies, rolls, sweets, and tea. We really didn't have many special things during the holidays like the English did," recalls Eithne Cunnane Cuckel of her childhood in County Mayo, Ireland. "We were too poor and didn't have the supplies. My dad called Christmas Eve 'Big Nuff'—the only night you got enough to eat! When he was small, currant buns were a treat—just plain bread with raisins.

"Since ours was a very small village, we didn't have midnight mass. Christmas morning we opened our presents and then were off to church. After dinner we sometimes were too full to cut the Christmas Cake. (p. 58) and saved it until 'Little Christmas' (January 6).

"Our first Christmas tree was very special," recalls Eithne. "An aunt sent us the lights. Making decorations and putting up the tree were all a part of the celebration. Dad built a little stable and crib (créche) for us. When Mother brought it out, we children gathered around for a rosary and carols. My brother Shamus played the piano."

Irish Boiled Fruit Cake

This is our traditional holiday cake, says Eithne Cuckel of Milpitas, California. The recipe comes from my mother, Kathleen Cunnane, who still lives in County Mayo, Ireland.

1 cup margarine
1 cup dark brown sugar
1 cup apple juice or
   hot water
½ cup prunes, chopped,
   or sultanas
1 cup dark raisins
1 cup golden raisins
¾ cup currants
½ cup dried apricots,
   chopped

½ cup candied cherries
¼ cup fresh orange
   peel, grated
½ cup dried fruit,
   chopped
3½ cups flour
½ tsp. baking soda
1¼ tsp. allspice
1¼ tsp. nutmeg
2 eggs, beaten
¼ cup blanched almonds,
   chopped

Butter a round, 9×3-inch spring-form pan or tube pan and line with greaseproof paper. Place margarine, sugar, apple juice or water (this cake is traditionally made with 1 cup Guinness Stout, in place of water, which enhances the flavor considerably), in a saucepan and bring to a boil, stirring until sugar dissolves and margarine is melted. Add mixed fruits and peel; then simmer over low heat for 3-5 minutes.

58

Remove from heat and cool to lukewarm. Sift flour, soda, and spices into large bowl. Make a well in center. Beat eggs and add to flour. Add cooled fruit mixture and almonds, mixing well. Turn into prepared tin and smooth top. Bake 1½–2 hours at 325° or until toothpick inserted comes out clean. Brush cake with white Karo syrup while hot and decorate with candied fruits and whole blanched almonds. Cool in tin. Wrap in foil. Store in covered container. Allow to mellow several weeks; cake improves with age.

o o o

In one part of Ireland Christmas Eve was called "The Night of the Cakes."

DUMB CAKES—While English men were dragging in the Yule log, women were busy cooking for Christmas Day. A traditional cake for Christmas Eve was the Dumb Cake which was made by single girls who wanted to know who their husbands were going to be. The young lady was forbidden to talk while she made the cake and put it in the oven. Then she was to open the door, and with some good luck, her future husband should walk into the kitchen at the stroke of midnight and turn the cake.

59

"Four to six weeks before Christmas we made this big basinful of fruit cake," says Marie Martinez, who grew up in Dublin, Ireland. "When all the ingredients were in, everyone had a go around with the spoon—if you could move it!—and made a wish. Later Mum topped the cake with royal icing and some fancy piping around the edge. We decorated the top with small ornaments. It was served at tea time on Christmas Day.

"Before Christmas Eve everyone was busy sprucing up the house. Curtains had to be washed, floors waxed. Dad would go out into the country to get holly and we hung it everywhere— along the wall, on the ledge over the doors, on top of pictures."

Marie's mother always put a two-foot candle in the window on Christmas Eve. According to an old Irish legend, the glow of the candles welcomed the Holy Family, who were said to be traveling the roads of the world. The tiny flickering lights, all over the countryside, invited anyone, who, like Joseph and Mary, might be looking for shelter.

"The day after Christmas—St. Stephen's Day—in Ireland we used to dress up in old rags and go from door to door begging for help to 'bury the wren' (always pronounced *wran*)," says Eithne Cuckel. "We sang, danced, or recited this poem for the lady of the house:

> The wran, the wran, the king of all birds,
> St. Stephen's Day he got caught in the furze (bushes).
> Though he's little, his family is great,
> Cheer up, good lady, and give us a treat!"

An old Irish legend describes a contest between an eagle and a skylark to see which could fly higher. A wren perched on the eagle's back; when the giant bird could fly no longer, the wren took off, soaring far above him.

St. Stephen's Day was called *Wrenning Day*, when they stoned a wren "in commemoration of St. Stephen, the first Christian martyr."

"For Christmas in Finland we always made *Joulotortut* (Yole-o-tor-tu), prune tarts," (p. 63), recalls Terttu Gilbert who grew up on a farm in that country. "The whole family helped Mother shape them in pinwheels and half moons. There was plenty of cutting and filling to be done, for 175 tarts were served to friends who came during the holidays. Mother also made a wreath of *pula,* our sweet bread filled with raisins and cardamom (the Christmas spice), and plenty of little round, spicy cookies called *piparkakut.* Some evenings we sipped hot berry drink made from black currants simmered with raisins, almonds, spices, and orange peel.

"Father usually butchered a pig in December so there was ham for Christmas dinner with prunes, apples, and boiled potatoes along with the traditional rice pudding with a hidden almond. The person finding it might get married that year; or if a young child, that person had to help with the dishes. My brother always swallowed the almond to escape that task.

"There were gifts to make for the whole family—Mother knitted and made dolls. Father built cars from wood for the boys. We made straw decorations for the tree and straw rams (*Joulopässi*) for the tables. Cleaning and baking started early; the house and barn had to be put in a 'Christmas condition.'"

—Terttu Gilbert is a mental health worker in San Jose, California.

Joulotortut
(Finnish Christmas Tarts)

½ lb. pitted prunes   1 tsp. lemon rind,
1 cup water   grated
Juice of ½ lemon   ¼ cup sugar
1 pkg. (17 oz.) frozen puff pastry° or frozen patty shells

Soak prunes until plump. Simmer in water until very soft. Add water as necessary. Mash to consistency of applesauce. Season with lemon and sugar; increase sugar if necessary.

Thaw 1 sheet puff pastry according to directions. Flour board, rolling pin. Roll pastry ⅛-inch thick. Cut in 4-inch circles, placing circles in refrigerator until ready to fill.

Wet edges of circles with water. Spoon 1 tsp. filling on one half of each circle. Fold over. Seal edges with prongs of a fork. Prick pastry. Brush with 1 egg beaten with 1 tbsp. water. Place on baking sheet. Bake at 450° for 8–10 minutes or until brown. Warm before serving.

° Frozen puff pastry sheets are available in frozen food sections of local supermarkets.

"In France we have lovely, religious manger scenes outside the churches. They are so popular that people come from outside of France to see them. Often you must wait in line a long time to see the crèche," recalls Elizabeth Thomas, of San Jose, California.

In Southern France it was the custom for the shepherd of a flock to bring a newborn lamb to the church for blessing on Christmas Eve. This tradition is still carried out at midnight mass in Les Baux (Provence), where men and women dressed as shepherds and shepherdesses form a candlelight procession to the church. A shepherd leads a small ceremonial cart festooned with candles and greenery bearing a white lamb to the altar.

Bûche de Noël
(French Christmas Log)

In France it is traditional to have thirteen desserts for Christmas dinner—walnuts, tangerines, dates, etc., but one of them must be the Bûche de Noël. The dessert is shaped like a yule log, filled and frosted with chocolate buttercream.

Cake Roll

- 6 egg yolks
- ½ cup sugar
- 1 tsp. vanilla
- ¼ tsp. salt
- ⅔ cup cake flour
- ½ tsp. baking powder
- 6 egg whites
- ¼ tsp. cream of tartar

Mocha Buttercream

- 1 cup sugar
- ⅓ cup water
- 2 eggs
- 2 tsp. vanilla
- 3 tsp. instant coffee
- 4 oz. unsweetened chocolate
- 1 cup sweet butter

Chocolate Meringue Buttercream

- 3 egg whites
- ¼ tsp. cream of tartar
- 1 cup sugar
- ⅓ cup water
- 2 tsp. vanilla
- 3 tsp. instant coffee
- 8 oz. semi-sweet chocolate
- 1 cup sweet butter

Cake Roll for Bûche de Noël: In mixer bowl beat yolks until light. Add sugar gradually and beat until very creamy. Blend in vanilla and salt. Sift cake flour, measure, and sift with baking powder. Gradually fold into egg yolk mixture. Beat whites until foamy; add cream of tartar and beat until stiff but not dry. Fold gently into egg yolk mixture. Spread in jelly roll pan greased and lined with wax paper. Bake at 400° 10–12 minutes or until golden and done. Immediately turn onto damp towel lined with wax paper under it. Peel paper from cake. Roll cake lengthwise in towel and wax paper and let cool at room temperature. Follow directions for constructing the Bûche with *either* mocha buttercream *or* chocolate meringue buttercream.

Mocha Buttercream: Beat eggs until light. Combine sugar and water in small saucepan and cook to soft-ball stage (234°). Beating constantly, gradually add to eggs and beat until cold. Add vanilla and coffee crystals and melted cooled chocolate. Gradually beat in room-temperature butter.

Chocolate Meringue Buttercream: Beat egg whites (room temperature) until foamy; add cream of tartar and beat at high speed until whites form stiff peaks. Combine sugar and water and boil until mixture forms a soft ball (234°). Slowly pour hot syrup into egg white mixture, beating constantly. Beat

66

at high speed for about 5 minutes, until mixture is cool, smooth, and satiny. Beat melted chocolate, coffee, and vanilla into cool meringue. Gradually beat in room-temperature butter. Chill until spreading consistency is reached.

Constructing the Bûche: Unroll cooled cake. Spread with half of the buttercream or meringue buttercream. Roll again and spread most of the remaining buttercream over top and sides. Slicing diagonally, cut off ends of cake. Frost with rest of buttercream and attach to cake to resemble knotholes on log. Use fork to make marks resembling bark across top of cake and knotholes. Decorate with holly leaves and berries made from marzipan (p. 55). Tint as desired with paste food coloring. Dust work surface with powdered sugar and roll marzipan thinly as possible. Cut with sharp knife. Set leaves on log to give three-dimensional effect. (For fluffier buttercream you may use about ⅓ margarine to ⅔ butter.)

Easy Bûche de Noël

Anne Marie Boube, of the French Consulate in San Francisco, loves to do gourmet cooking on weekends. She suggests this log "which is easy and suitable when you have to cook a large meal because it doesn't take long to prepare."

1 lb. tin chestnut purée°	3 tbsp. strong coffee
4 oz. semi-sweet chocolate	6 tbsp. sweet butter
⅔ cup powdered sugar	Powdered sugar
	Whipped cream

Mash chestnut purée to soften. Melt chocolate; add powdered sugar, butter, chestnut purée, and coffee. Mix with wooden spoon until very smooth.

Pour chocolate mixture onto sheet of foil and form into shape of a log. Refrigerate. Place log on serving plate. With prongs of a fork, trace lines to resemble bark of a tree. Sprinkle with powdered sugar to resemble snow. Serve with side serving of whipped cream.

° Imported from France, chestnut purée is available in specialty food stores.

The Cake of the Kings

"Our Christmas season in France comes to an end on Epiphany (January 6) when we commemorate the coming of the three kings to Bethlehem," says Elizabeth Thomas. "Everyone celebrates this day—even the schools.

"The special attraction which concludes every Twelfth Night dinner is the *Galette des Rois*, the cake of the kings. Inside the galette is a bean, or good-luck charm called *fève*. The one finding the charm becomes king for the evening and he may choose a queen. We do it at home and the kids love it."

A golden paper crown tops the *galette* when it comes to the table, along with a silver crown for the queen. Often they are made by one of the children in the family. If the cake comes from a bakery, the baker sends the traditional crowns.

In some parts of France, expecially Normandy, children go about singing traditional Twelfth Night carols.

Other countries have similar customs—like the almond in the Christmas Eve rice dish in Scandinavia, the sixpence in the English Christmas pudding, the gold coin in Greek *Vasilopita*, and Mexican families search for a bean or tiny doll in their *Rosca de los Reyes* to bring good fortune.

Galette des Rois
(Cake of the Kings)

From Northern France and Paris comes this cake for Epiphany.
Marthe Nussbaumer of Alsace bakes this almond-filled pastry
for the holiday.

2 eggs
¾ cup powdered sugar
4 tbsp. soft butter
2 tbsp. lemon rind,
     grated
1 tbsp. lemon juice or
     kirsch

1 cup + 3 tbsp.
     ground almonds or
     filberts, , or 1 cup
     + 3 tbsp. almond
     powder, or 1 can
     (8 oz.) almond paste
Dry bean or fève
Egg glaze

½ pkg. (17-oz.) frozen puff pastry

Thaw puff pastry according to directions. Flour board and rolling pin; roll out. Cut 2 10-inch circles and place 1 circle on baking sheet, flan, or pie pan. Spread filling evenly over pastry,
leaving ¾-inch border. Place bean or fève in any part of paste.
Wet edges of circle with water. Cover filling with top circle of
puff pastry. Seal firmly and crimp edges. Brush with an egg
lightly beaten. With fine point of knife make diamond designs

over top of pastry. Prick dough well with fork prongs. Cover with plastic wrap and chill well. Bake at 400° for 20 minutes. Cool before serving.

Filling: Beat sugar and eggs until thick and lemon-colored. Add butter, ground nuts, or powder, or almond paste, lemon rind, and flavoring. Mix well.

From gold and silver foil or other paper, make crowns for king and queen. Present cake topped with king's crown.

The center of the French Christmas celebration is the crèche, or manger scene. Every home will have its own with tiny clay figures called *santons* (little saints).

After midnight mass on Christmas Eve comes the *réveillon*, the late supper that is the big event of the season. In Alsace, goose is the main dish—in Brittany, buckwheat cakes with sour cream. Burgundy feasts on turkey and chestnuts, while Paris enjoys its *pâté de foie gras*.

Gifts are exchanged at New Year's.

71

72

EVERYWHERE IN GERMANY the four weeks of Advent are looked upon as a time of preparation for the greatest festival of the Christian year.

Children happily make their own Christmas greetings, while mothers and grandmothers knit furiously to finish the last mittens, caps, and stockings. Fathers may carve or build toys for young children. And from every kitchen comes the sweet aroma of spicy ginger cookies, cakes, and tortes baking for the big celebration, Christmas Day.

On Sundays, in both homes and churches, Advent wreaths with their four candles are lit, one for each Sunday. In the dusk of the late afternoon families gather around the wreath and the warm fire to play the piano and sing carols. Coffee is served, and Mother proudly brings out the first Christmas cookies for everyone to sample and "see how they turned out."

Christmas Kugelhopf

This delightful holiday cake/bread is traditionally baked in a *Kugelhopf* mold. Decorated with small red candles and holly leaves, it becomes a festive offering for a Christmas brunch or tea. Originating in Austria, *Kugelhopf* (also known as *Gugelhupf* or *Napfkuchen*) is popular in France, Germany, and Switzerland as well.

1 pkg. active dry yeast	1 tsp. salt
½ cup lukewarm water	1 tsp. vanilla
1 tsp. sugar	Grated peel of 1 lemon
1 cup sweet butter, softened	4 cups flour
2/3 cup sugar	1 cup golden raisins
6 eggs	½ cup slivered almonds
	Powdered sugar

Dissolve yeast in warm water and 1 tsp. sugar. Cream butter and sugar; add salt, lemon rind, vanilla, and eggs, one at a time, beating well after each addition. Add yeast mixture and gradually add 2 cups sifted flour. Beat hard with electric mixer for 5 minutes. Gradually add remaining flour and continue beating until dough is elastic. Stir in raisins. Turn into greased bowl; cover with a towel and let rise in warm place until doubled in bulk (about 1½-2 hours). Stir dough down; add almonds. Spoon into well-greased and floured 10-inch *Kugelhopf* mold or tube pan.

Cover and let rise in warm place until batter comes within ½ inch of top of mold (about 1 hour). Bake at 475° for 10 minutes; reduce heat to 350° and continue baking for about 40-45 minutes or until cake tester comes out clean. Let stand in pan 5 minutes before turning out on cooling rack. Before serving, dust with powdered sugar. Decorate with small red birthday-size candles and holders, holly leaves, and berries. Serve warm with fresh butter.

Greek Vasilopita

Baked by every housewife and village baker, this traditional cake honors Basil, the patron saint of the Greek New Year. Decorated with numerals of the coming year and baked with a hidden coin inside, the *Vasilopita* is cut exactly at the stroke of midnight. Aristea Pettis, San Jose, California, shares this recipe from her treasure of Greek cooking.

2 pkg. active dry yeast	2 tsp. orange rind, grated
½ cup warm water	2 tsp. mahlep° (optional) or 1 tsp. cardamom
1 tsp. sugar	
½ cup milk	
¾ cup sugar	½ tsp. salt
⅔ cup butter	5-5½ cups flour
3 eggs	Egg glaze, Sesame seed

Grind the mahlep. Dissolve yeast in warm water and sugar. Heat milk, butter, and ¾ cup sugar over medium heat until dissolved. Pour into large mixing bowl. When lukewarm, add yeast mixture, slightly beaten eggs, orange rind, salt, and spice. Gradually add half the flour and beat 5 minutes with electric mixer. Gradually add 2-2½ cups flour as necessary. Turn out onto lightly floured board and knead until smooth and elastic, about 8–10 minutes. Place in greased bowl, turning to grease top of dough. Cover and set in warm place until double in bulk.

Knead a second time; cover and let rise again. Punch down and return dough to bowl for a *third* rising. Punch down and shape into a round ball, reserving a small piece the size of a lime for decoration. Pat into 10-inch spring-form pan. Cover and let stand in warm place until almost double in bulk.

On floured board, roll small piece of dough into pencil-thin rope, adding extra flour. Cut in 4 pieces and shape numbers of coming year. Lay gently on top of cake. Brush with 1 egg beaten with 1 tbsp. water. Traditionally, the top is sprinkled with black and white sesame seeds (available in Greek delis). Bake at 350° for about 45 minutes or until hollow-sounding when tapped. Makes 1 large loaf. Cut in thirds across loaf and slice in ½-inch pieces.

°Mahlep, a Middle Eastern spice made from the kernel of black cherries, adds fragrance and sweetness to baking. A Greek baker suggests using 1 tsp. ground cardamom or coriander as a substitute. Greek delis carry mahlep.

IN GREECE, gifts are exchanged on St. Basil's Day rather than Christmas, which is a religious celebration. A special cake (p. 76) is baked with a coin inside in remembrance of Basil, who is known for his generosity to the poor. He is said to have helped orphaned and destitute young girls with their dowries by slipping coins into little cakes, then tossing them through the window at night.

New Year's Eve is an important family evening when even the youngest may stay up, joining in games and storytelling until midnight. When church bells chime at twelve o'clock, the father slices the *Vasilopita* (Vas-i-*low*-pita) with pieces for the church, the poor, the eldest in the family, and on down. Pieces are quickly torn apart in search of the coin which brings good luck for the rest of the year.

In some places families take the *Vasilopita* to the church for a priestly blessing before the family gathering.

IN MEXICO children believe the wise men bring their gifts on Three Kings' Day, or Epiphany (January 6). "On that evening children put out water and hay for the wise men's camels," recalls Rosa Cavillo of San Jose, California, "and we set our shoes on the windowsill, hoping for gifts from the kings. The presents were little things—like a brush and comb, or a bracelet, but they were very special to us.

"Mother baked the traditional Three Kings' Cake (p. 80) in the shape of a ring or crown which she used as a centerpiece for our big dinner. The honor of cutting the cake went to my grandmother."

Inside the cake is a small china doll or bean. The person finding it becomes king or queen for the meal, but that person is also obligated to host a party or supper on Candlemas, February 2. Sometimes the finder, not feeling quite so lucky, quickly swallows the bean.

Mexican Rosca de los Reyes

Three Kings' Cake is a fruit and nut filled ring or crown topped with icing and decorations. It is traditional for Three Kings' Day in Mexico.

2 pkgs. active dry yeast	1 tsp. orange peel, grated
½ cup lukewarm water	4–5 cups flour
1 tsp. sugar	½ cup raisins
⅔ cup milk	½ cup candied orange peel, chopped
4 tbsp. butter	¼ cup candied red and green cherries, chopped
¼ cup sugar	½ cup walnuts, chopped
½ tsp. salt	Glaze
3 eggs	
1 tsp. lemon peel, grated	

Dissolve yeast and sugar in warm water. Over medium heat, warm milk, butter, sugar, and salt. Cool to lukewarm. Beat eggs until light. Add orange and lemon peel, milk and yeast mixtures to eggs. Gradually add 2½ cups flour. Beat 5 minutes with electric mixer. Add 1-1½ cups flour, as necessary. Turn out onto floured board and knead until smooth and elastic, about 8–10 minutes. Carefully work in fruit and nuts, distributing evenly. Place in greased bowl, turning to grease top of dough. Cover and let rise in warm place until double in bulk. Punch down.

On lightly floured surface, divide dough in half, roll into 2 26-inch ropes. Form ring and seal ends together. Place on greased baking sheet. Cover and let rise until almost double. Bake at 375° for 10 minutes. Cover with foil and bake 10–15 minutes more. Cool. Cut triangular wedge from cake ring and insert bean or tiny doll. Replace wedge. Glaze with mixture of powdered sugar, cream, and vanilla. Decorate with candied fruits and walnut halves. Sometimes in Mexico glazed orange slices are used as decoration.

Light Christmas Cake from Warsaw

5 eggs
2 cups confectioners' sugar
1 cup butter
3 tsp. lemon peel, grated
1 tsp. vanilla
¼ cup orange juice
3 cups cake flour
2 tsp. baking powder
½ tsp. salt
¼ cup candied orange rind, diced
½ cup prunes, diced
½ cup figs or dates, diced
¾ cup walnuts, chopped
¾ cup currants or raisins

Prepare fruit and nuts. Sprinkle with 2 tbsp. of the flour; sift remaining flour with baking powder and salt. Beat eggs until light and lemon-colored. Cream butter, lemon peel, and vanilla until fluffy. Beat in orange juice, eggs and mix. Gradually add flour mixture and beat well. Fold in fruit and nuts. Turn batter into generously greased and floured 10–inch tube pan (or two 8×4×3–inch loaf pans). Bake at 350° 1 hour or until cake tester comes out clean. Cool cake in pan 10 minutes; turn onto wire rack. Spread with lemon glaze.

Lemon Glaze: 1 cup powdered sugar, 2 tbsp. lemon juice, ½ tsp. grated lemon peel mixed.

A Polish Christmas Eve (Wigilia) Supper

Early in the day the father brings in clean straw to lay under the white tablecloth—a reminder of Christ's stable. Mother sets out her best dishes and sets an extra place for an unexpected guest. Polish people believe a guest in the home is God in the home. Food is ready and waiting in the kitchen. Excitement fills the cozy, warm home.

When finally the first star appears in the evening sky, the father calls his family to share the *oplatek* (holy bread of love), a wafer blessed by the priest. Happy is their time together, sharing the twelve special Christmas dishes, singing, and storytelling around the table until the church bells ring at 11:00. Then father readies horses and sleigh for the family to attend mass—the shepherd's watch.

It is the belief in some villages that while the congregation prays, peace descends on the snow covered earth and the humble animals, at home in the barn, are given the power to speak—but only the innocent of heart may hear them.

—*From remembrances of Vera Kawulka, Santa Clara, California.*

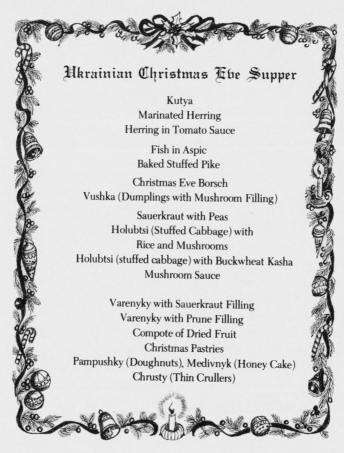

Ukrainian Christmas Eve Supper

Kutya
Marinated Herring
Herring in Tomato Sauce

Fish in Aspic
Baked Stuffed Pike

Christmas Eve Borsch
Vushka (Dumplings with Mushroom Filling)

Sauerkraut with Peas
Holubtsi (Stuffed Cabbage) with
Rice and Mushrooms
Holubtsi (stuffed cabbage) with Buckwheat Kasha
Mushroom Sauce

Varenyky with Sauerkraut Filling
Varenyky with Prune Filling
Compote of Dried Fruit
Christmas Pastries
Pampushky (Doughnuts), Medivnyk (Honey Cake)
Chrusty (Thin Crullers)

Ukrainian Medivnyk

(Honey Cake)

Honey cakes are very much a part of the Ukrainian and Polish Christmas tradition. Lil Proceviat, Mountain View, California, shares her recipe for the true honey lover. Lil prefers the cake plain, enjoying the flavor and aroma of the honey. For best results, she suggests using only buckwheat or a dark, high quality honey. This is a beautiful, light cake.

6	eggs	2	tsp. baking soda
1	cup sugar	¼	tsp. salt
1	cup buckwheat honey	1	tsp. cinnamon
1	cup safflower oil	1	tsp. cloves
1	cup buttermilk	3	cups flour

Beat eggs until light and lemon-colored. Add sugar gradually and mix well. Add honey and oil; cream thoroughly. Combine buttermilk and soda; add to mixture and beat well. Add spices, salt, and gradually add sifted flour. Pour into a well-greased and floured tube or bundt pan. Bake at 350° 1½ hours or until done. Cool 10 minutes in pan and remove to rack. (½ cup chopped walnuts and ⅜ cup chopped raisins may be added to the batter after the addition of flour, if you wish.) Cake stored in airtight container improves with age. May be served with whipped cream.

IN THE UKRAINE the Christmas celebration begins when the first star appears in the evening sky, says Marie Halun Bloch. Usually the children watch for it and call out, "There's the Christmas star!"

Before we sat down to the Christmas Eve meal, my father had prepared black bread sliced very thin and spread with comb honey. Starting with my Mother, he stood in front of her and made a little speech of Christmas wishes. He mentioned all the things he hoped would happen for Mother during the coming year. Then Mother made a little speech to Father and they kissed each other and took a slice of bread and honey. Father did this for each of the children. The younger ones always kissed his hand and gave him a hug before eating their bread.

Mother's table was festive with straw under the embroidered

cloth in remembrance of the manger. A place was set at the table for missing family members or an unexpected guest. Sometimes in rural areas a sheaf of wheat was brought in. Family members considered it an abode for the spirits of ancestors, who, it was believed, returned twice a year to check on their welfare.

Traditionally there were twelve courses at the meal, symbolizing the twelve apostles. However, the most important place at the table was given to a large bowl of *kutya*, made of whole grain wheat boiled with poppy seeds, nuts, figs, dates, and honey. No table was complete without this dish for it signified a plentiful harvest. Everyone took a spoonful of *kutya* and of the other twelve dishes as well. Everything one did at Christmas symbolized the ancient birthday.

Ours was a quiet, thoughtful meal, remembering Christmases past. When we had finished everyone joined in singing carols. There was no visiting on Christmas Eve and no emphasis on gifts. At midnight the family went to the candlelight church service that sometimes lasted three or four hours.

On Christmas Eve a lighted candle was placed in the window an invitation to any homeless stranger to join in celebrating the birth of Christ.

—*Marie Halun Bloch, Denver, Colorado, is the author of seventeen books for children. She has written of a childhood Christmas in her book*, Marya.

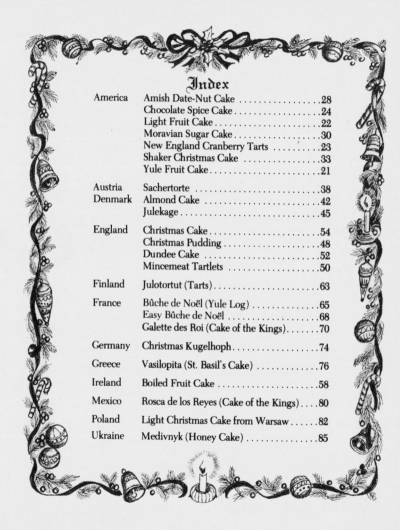

Index